AUTISM:

Unpacking the Puzzle

(Oh the Possibilities)

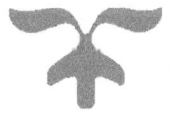

Stephanie L. Gooden

Autism: Unpacking the Puzzle (Oh the Possibilities)

Copyright © 2021 by Stephanie L. Gooden

All rights reserved. No part of this publication may be reproduced, distributed, or transmitted in any form or by any means, including photocopying, recording, or other electronic to mechanical methods, without the prior written permission of the publisher, except in the case of brief quotation embodied in reviews and certain other non-commercial uses permitted by copyright law. For permission requests, write to the publisher at the below email address.

gooden.stephanie@gmail.com

Paperback ISBN: 978-0-578-86999-5

Digital (ebook) ISBN: 978-0-578-86998-8

This book is dedicated to my precious son and daughter and all the parents and caregivers around the world who were blessed to parent a child with autism.

In this book, you will receive first-hand information on raising a child(ren) with autism and my personal journey of unpacking the puzzle.

TABLE OF CONTENTS

Chapter 1: The Beginning 4

Chapter 2: After the Birth 7

Chapter 3: The Early Months 11

Chapter 4: What Changed? 13

Chapter 5: Early Intervention 16

Chapter 6: Gotta have tough skin! 20

Chapter 7: The Official Diagnosis 24

Chapter 8: Applied Behavioral Analysis. What we are learning 27

Chapter 9: 8 Tips for Your Child's Individualized Educational Plan (IEP) 30

Chapter 10: Adding a Sibling to the Equation 34

Chapter 11: Things I wish I knew as a new parent 37

Chapter 12: You can't pour from an empty cup. 41

Appendix I: Question & Answers Unpacking a bit more 43

Appendix II: My promise to myself as a caregiver 50

Chapter 1:

The Beginning

(Trigger warning)

As a first-time mom pregnant with my son, I remember being overjoyed when I saw the "You are pregnant" sign on the pregnancy test. It was Thanksgiving Day. Just six months prior, I had experienced a miscarriage at five weeks of gestation. I remember not wanting to tell anyone about this pregnancy due to the hurt from my previous pregnancy. Finally, I said to myself, Stephanie, you deserve to be a mom. You deserve to have a family. My boyfriend was just as excited. He later became my fiancé a few months after finding out we were expecting again.

Picking out cute baby clothes, deciding on the nursery's theme, picking out a name, and reading baby books was just the start of it. It was time for us to go to the ultrasound appointment to find out the gender. I remember tears falling down my cheeks as I reclined on the table for the ultrasound. I began to have flashbacks from my previous pregnancy.

With my previous pregnancy, I learned about my miscarriage while at my first ultrasound appointment. My boyfriend and I went to an ultrasound room like this one. I laid down on the table - excited and nervous. We watched as the sonographer used the transducer to press against my stomach. At first, she moved the transducer from right to left. Soon it appeared as if she couldn't get a clear image, so I thought. Then she asked could she do a vaginal ultrasound? Of course, I said yes. She used the vaginal transducer and then said, "I can't find a heartbeat." I will never forget that moment. It felt like a ton of bricks on top of my chest, and all the air left my lungs. I began to cry in utter disbelief. I remember hearing the empty sound from the ultrasound microphone as she moved the transducer around. No heartbeat, just motionless fluid. A microphone sound without any movement. The doctor came into the room a bit later to comfort us and answer some of my "why" questions. She ultimately told us that my pregnancy had terminated itself.

Now, months later, and choosing a different doctor this go-round, I'm in the ultrasound room (four months pregnant) about to find out the gender. We were both so excited just to be blessed to be at this point. This pregnancy was accompanied by receiving daily progesterone suppositories for up to six months due to bleeding and then, plagued with pre-eclampsia at seven months. Before starting the ultrasound, I asked the sonographer to turn off the volume. I was afraid to hear the same sound of emptiness if, in fact, this pregnancy was like the last. I also chose to turn my head away from the screen so that I could not see anything. As she began, I asked her was the baby moving and was there a heartbeat. She smiled and replied, "yes." Then asked, "do you want to know the gender?" She announced that we were having a baby boy. I looked at my boyfriend as he smiled from ear-to-ear. She counted his hands, feet and took other images. My baby boy was perfect, now finally turning to look at the screen. She then asked, "do you want to hear his heartbeat?" and with tears rolling down my cheeks - tears of joy - I said yes.

My precious boy was born at 35 weeks via cesarean section. The pre-eclampsia had gotten the best of me, which caused an earlier birth. I wasn't mentally prepared to deliver via C-section. My baby's heartbeat began to slow down, my blood pressure began to rise, so the best option for both of us was to have an early delivery. His dad and I welcomed a healthy baby boy just two days after the Fourth of July.

CHAPTER 2:

AFTER THE BIRTH

Bringing my precious baby home, breastfeeding, changing diapers, and washing clothes at first was overwhelming. We're talking about first-time parents living in a state with no family nearby. We brought all the new baby items: a bouncer, swing, rocker, and was ready to take on parenthood. Moreover, little did I know our faith was about to be tested.

Three-weeks postpartum, I began to experience extreme pains in my chest and had to be admitted to the hospital. After yet another ultrasound, I was diagnosed with gallstones while in the ER. I needed to have surgery, the doctor told me. The doctor said the surgery is routine and would consist of a very short hospital stay. However, the surgery turned out to be a total nightmare but also my best testimony. After the laparoscopic surgery to remove my gallbladder, I began to feel very weak directly after coming from the recovery room. That same night, while in my hospital room, I told my nurse how I felt, and he replied that it was normal for someone to feel weak after surgery. That night I attempted to walk to the bathroom, and the last thing I remember is hitting my head against the bathroom wall before blacking out.

I woke up in a cold sweat in a bright room filled with what seemed to be a million doctors and nurses. I asked them what happened, and no one responded. I overheard my nurse on the phone in the hallway with my fiancé, telling him that they found me unresponsive on the floor and that he needed to come to the hospital quickly.

Being placed in the ICU immediately afterward, I remember being so scared. I had just given birth in this same hospital a few weeks ago. Now here I am laying in the ICU with all types of machines hooked to me. Could this be real?

The doctors stated that I appeared to have internal bleeding. Later, I found out that the bleeding was coming from the incision site from surgery and two other spots. I was never told by the surgeon that conducted my surgery that they had nicked my liver. I found out what happened from my sister and fiancé when they asked the hospital staff what happened. My hemoglobin was critically low due to internal bleeding. I was given ten blood transfusions, and even then, my hemoglobin increased very little. While in the ICU, I had to have two additional surgeries. One surgery resulted in them placing a temporary peg tube attached to my stomach to collect the blood floating inside.

I awake from my second surgery, and my family from Detroit (sister, dad, two aunts, and cousin) had flown in to be by my bedside and pray for me. My baby's first time meeting his only aunt and grandfather was during this tragic event. While in the ICU, my health didn't immediately improve after the surgeries. I honestly thought God was taking me away to be with him. My family, fiancé, and his mother prayed for and encouraged me not to give up. Even the doctors (not the surgeon) came to my bedside to tell me how they gathered downstairs to say a prayer for me.

While in the ICU the assigned hematologist informed me that I was a hemophiliac. My pregnancy supposedly caused the condition. I never had blood clotting issues my whole life, so this was hard to understand. It was all too much! My family and fiancé's mom stayed to assist my fiancé with our newborn and be with me. I gained strength from having my loved ones near, and I believe that their prayers aided in my healing. I remember one of my aunts and cousin coming into my hospital room in the ICU, making me laugh so hard that it elevated my heart rate. I had to explain to the doctors the next day why my heart rate jumped at certain times due to my family making me laugh trying to lift my spirits.

My sister, who is a registered nurse, stayed with me all night near my bedside and gave all the ICU nurses a run for their money. When I was finally discharged from the ICU to a regular surgical floor, I believe all the nurses were happy to see me leave. It was so funny to see my sister looking at my medical charts and getting the doctors to order additional tests. You would have sworn she was at her place of employment. I did not have an appetite, not sure if it was due to the blood loss, so I went days without eating anything. To get me to have some type of nutrients, the nurses made me veggie smoothies. It wasn't until my family came that I tried to eat something, so I started by sipping on broth.

Being hospitalized caused me not to attend my baby's first-month doctor appointment, which really crushed my spirits. Before being discharged from the hospital, I had to be cleared by the cardiologist, pulmonologist, hematologist, and other specialists. After a little over two weeks, I was discharged. Having to self-medicate with over seven different medications was hard, but I'd take anything over being in a hospital setting. Imagine having to spend weeks of maternity leave in the hospital and the following months having to go to follow-up appointments. Although the first year after giving birth was blighted with monthly hematology and ER visits due to the bleeding disorder, nothing compared to taking care of my baby boy.

CHAPTER 3:

THE EARLY MONTHS

Everything appeared to be okay. We brought toys with sweet melodies, bright lights, and silly songs. I watched my baby smile and babble. We danced to music, took pictures, and recorded videos to commemorate his milestones. By three-months-old, he had his first smile, began to lift his head, and had the cutest little laugh.

By six-months-old, he began to roll on his sides, grab for his pacifier and toys, and began to babble a bit more. Seven-months-old, he began to sit up by himself. We took our first visit to Zoo Miami at nine-months-old, and he was so happy. Also, at month nine, he began to stand more frequently. He was a pro at holding his sippy cup and began to eat solid foods. For his first trip to the beach, we planned to take his nine-month-old pictures. We learned then that he hated the water splashing on his legs. No crawling yet, but he now began to clap his hands to certain songs and on command. He was so silly, always laughing and smiling.

At 10-months-old, he began to take 4-5 steps unassisted. He also stood for long periods. By 11-months, my boy was full fledge walking. At this age, he became intrigued with watching cartoons. At 12-months-old, he loved to go for walks and understood directives. He had two first birthday parties (one in Florida where we resided and the other in Detroit, where our families live). In months 13 to-18, we introduced him to playing in the pool, sliding and swinging at the park, eating more table foods, scribbling with crayons, and his first haircut.

CHAPTER 4:

WHAT CHANGED?

When my son turned 19-20 months old, I began to notice a difference in his responses and behaviors. Around 20-months-old, I remember he had a routine doctor's appointment that we attended, and they completed a developmental assessment. I remember the pediatrician asking me, "does your child wave bye-bye?" I thought to myself at first, then responded, "no." She replied, "You better start working on him waving bye before he gets diagnosed." Those words haunted me. Diagnosed; diagnosed with what? After that appointment, I went home and researched what it could mean when a child isn't waving goodbye at his age. One of the first headings that came up was Autism Spectrum Disorder. I was in disbelief, shocked, and confused. No, there is no way my little boy could have autism. He smiles and laughs, I said to myself.

Although he had good eye-contact until recently, I felt what I was reading online had to be a mistake. But no one in my family was autistic. I began to think - how could this be. At 20-months-old, I researched some of the milestones that children his age should be doing: pretend play, running, and jumping. My son did none of these yet. Upon further research and what caused me to act were the signs that I'd observed in my child's behaviors that were signs associated with autism:

- hand flapping
- lining up toys
- spinning around in the circle
- walking on his tippy toes
- regression in speech
- repetitive words, phrases, and sounds

- covering his ears
- avoiding play with other children
- unresponsiveness to his name
- social withdrawal
- lack of eye-contact
- overly focused on one specific toy (i.e., spinning toys)
- he could not point to items

After viewing and discussing many of these behaviors with my fiancé, I felt both of us went through a grieving period. My fiancé expressed the grieving stage of denial while I went straight to the grieving stage of anger. Being a woman of faith, I questioned God. I spoke to him, "Lord, why would you allow this to happen? Why? You know my story, the miscarriage, my health scare, things that happened in my childhood, and now you allow this." I was so angry without getting an official autism diagnosis, but I knew it was something I could not deny.

After a period of grief, I thought to myself, you've cried about it; now it's time to get into action. Having a background in child welfare case management, I was knowledgeable of the next steps. You would have to get your child referred for an early intervention assessment. One morning I woke up and called to make an appointment with the early intervention agency.

CHAPTER 5:

EARLY INTERVENTION

After the early intervention agency's initial assessment, my son was assigned a developmental therapist who worked with his communication skills at daycare and home. We were assigned a service coordinator to monitor the services, which were comparable to a case manager. By this time, he was about twenty-one months old; my fiancé and I chose to place him in a different daycare as we observed the teaching staff's lack of care. One teacher even said that she liked my child because he was quiet and easy. After seeing some red flags, we chose to transfer him into a different daycare with cameras to monitor him in class while we were at work.

Not only did the developmental therapist work with him, but she also worked with us and provided valuable knowledge, and suggested many items (i.e., toys and videos) to assist with his growth and development. However, even with this therapy, I felt he also needed speech therapy. His pediatrician agreed and provided a referral for him to receive speech therapy. When I brought my concerns to our assigned service coordinator from the early intervention agency, she stated that they did not take pediatricians' recommendations. She said that his assigned therapist could recommend a speech consultation after seeing him for three months and if she feels there was no noticeable progress.

Then I was informed by the service coordinator that if I wanted my child to have speech therapy, I should get it through my health insurance as the speech consultations they provide would only join a session every three months. I asked could we at least get the speech consultation on board now, and it was approved. After the speech consultation was added to his services, she completed the consultation at his daycare center. The developmental therapist and I were both present at the consultation. The therapist informed the speech consultant about my son's behaviors, how he memorizes certain letters of the alphabet and the fact that he covers his ears to certain sounds. In my opinion, they were giving cues to one another; although they never mentioned it verbally, they felt my child was autistic. Possibly not wanting me to worry. Something in my gut told me to move forward in paying for a private speech therapist to get the ball rolling. I then found a therapy agency through my insurance, and my son completed a speech evaluation. The evaluation results recommended speech therapy three times a week and occupational therapy (OT) twice a week. I forwarded the evaluation and recommendations to the service coordinator, and I wrote the following email to her:

"Hello, I just wanted to give you an update on my son. Along with his speech evaluation recommending speech therapy three times a week, we also completed the recommended OT evaluation, which was recommended twice a week. We are currently paying out of pocket, which has caused great hardship, and I have gotten a second job just to pay for both therapies. I am pleading that if you could add even one or two speech therapy sessions to his case, we would graciously appreciate it. I understand that your agency's fiscal does not start over until the middle of the year, so it may be due to financial difficulties in paying for sessions, but my child is regressing. He has forgotten words he used to know and is showing additional signs of autism. We currently have a Neurology appointment in July (due to their waiting list), but I am desperately asking for assistance. It breaks my heart, knowing that I cannot give him the services he needs because I can't afford them. Especially now with two jobs and his dad is working overtime. Please can you do whatever you can?"

One afternoon while sitting in the waiting area for my son to finish speech therapy, I began talking to the other parents. We begin to share our stories right there in the waiting room. One of the parents told me she noticed every time I came into the center, I paid out of pocket and asked why the early intervention agency was not covering the payments. She explained how she had to advocate for additional services aggressively and demanded an autism assessment for her child. I informed her that I had done the same thing; that's when she told me she had to escalate her concerns to some of the head people in charge.

After having that conversation, I was honestly so motivated and determined. I chose to take my requests for additional services a step further. Let's just say my child now received all his services and qualified for the autism assessment. Since I chose one of the therapy providers under the early intervention umbrella when I was paying out of pocket, he was able to keep that same speech and occupational therapist. We were also assigned a new service coordinator.

While participating in the services, my fiancé and I began to see so much improvement. All the services made a world of difference. After completing the paperwork to request the autism assessment through early intervention, we felt he also needed assistance to address our concerns regarding his social, emotional, and behavioral skills. If you find yourself debating whether or not to have your child assessed for early intervention therapies, know it cannot harm, only help. This service is free, and all the therapies listed under it are at no cost. Remember, the longer you wait, the more your child will miss out on learning some of the necessary skills needed to function.

CHAPTER 6:

GOTTA HAVE TOUGH SKIN!

The autism assessment was scheduled through one of the early intervention agency providers. We were there for about 2-3 hours. Most of the evaluation was an observation of how our child played, responded to toys, and his reactions. Our service coordinator was present in the building, although she did not observe the assessment. When the evaluation was over, I sent the following email to our service coordinator:

"May 17th:

Hello,

I just want to thank you so much for your kindness today. We walked in feeling hopeful about how to care for our son but leaving the evaluation we felt attacked and confused. The assessor/ owner seemed to be offended that I wanted my child to have all the services and not just behavioral as she repeated multiple times - "so you're picking them over us." This journey has been very hard having to experience many providers with many different opinions, but I digested it all because I want the very best for my baby. Today was very hard. Luckily the speech therapist warned us that this evaluation would be tough. It appeared that the assessor was trying to schedule my son for one session at home and the other at school, which was fine. I didn't get a chance to request if he could have behavioral services twice a week because I know that he needs it, and every parent at the therapy agency told me how helpful it is for the ITDS (Infant Toddler Developmental Specialist) to come twice a week.

The assessor/ owner appeared to develop an opinion insisting that we were choosing them (meaning speech and OT) over her agency which only provided behavioral therapy. She felt that her agency provided the best ABA (Applied Behavioral Analysis) services, and my son wouldn't need any other therapy.

As she said goodbye and opened the door, she repeated herself, saying, "so you're choosing them over us." We never chose speech and OT over them. I wanted my son to have all the available services. It seemed like I could request ABA twice a week, but she let her ego take over the assessment. I feel very confused and could really use some guidance. Any assistance you could provide would be helpful. She has to realize that with our previous experience with the ITDS, the therapist came out inconsistently, and we have not seen her in over a month. We are so happy to have consistent services at the therapy agency that provides speech and OT that we don't want to lose them. The prior ITDS had a lot going on in her personal life, which seemed to consume her time to where she would miss some weeks for the very short period we had her. Could you please help us with this?"

We had to develop a tough skin. The assessment was extremely hard as this was the first time hearing the words "your child appears to be autistic" by a professional. Although I already knew in my heart, it just felt like a weight had been lifted off me. Did it help that the assessor lacked any emotion or empathy in her delivery? Absolutely not! But now I knew what was going on with my son. After all of this, my son was now receiving all three therapies: speech, occupational, and Applied Behavioral Analysis (ABA). As a parent of any child with or without developmental delays or disabilities, you have to advocate for them. I found that there are so many professionals who will give their opinions on what they feel is right for your child, but you have to stand up and speak up on what you think is best to help your child.

My fiancé and I made a schedule of which one of us would take our son to therapy on a specific day, and we turned our apartment into a work center to assist our child with communication. Words and labels were everywhere. Each day for at least an hour, we would implement whatever he was learning in the three therapies at home. One of the best things I found that worked, which the ABA therapist suggested, was placing all of our son's favorite items inside a clear storage bin and putting the bin in clear view but out of his reach. This sort of forced him to begin to request things like his cup and toys. It was so awesome to see his progress in commencing to communicate.

It's hard to see your child cry and have tantrums because they can't communicate their wants and needs. It's also hard trying to guess if something or someone is bothering them. While ABA through early intervention was beneficial, we knew that all services would end once he turned 3-years-old. We begin looking early for different providers who accepted our insurance. If faced with this dilemma, start searching for services as early as possible to find a provider that you and your child are comfortable with.

CHAPTER 7:

THE OFFICIAL DIAGNOSIS

At two and a half years old, we went to see the pediatric neurologist who officially diagnosed our son with Autism Spectrum Disorder (F 84.0). The delay was due to a very long waitlist in making the appointment to see an excellent pediatric neurologist. This neurologist was the second doctor we saw, as the first one we found did not answer our questions and had very odd techniques. Every doctor is not for everyone. If you feel that a doctor you go to is not right for you, parents, please know that you have every right to find a different health professional who answers all of your questions. Even if you feel you need a second opinion, know that you and your child deserve a thorough and clear care plan.

At this point, I was moving toward acceptance. His dad, on the other hand, stayed in denial for some time before shifting to acceptance. We both were extremely engaged in his therapies. Receiving his official diagnosis made me shed a few tears, but this time of relief. The pediatric neurologist was compassionate, which is something his dad and I needed. The neurology team conducted an autism evaluation assessment, which took a little over an hour, and they asked us a lot of questions about our day-to-day with our son.

Most of the questions were geared towards his attention span, understanding/comprehension, and communication skills. The neurologist asked what services were my son currently receiving and when we told her the lists of therapies, she said that those were all the therapies she was going to recommend. She advised us to continue each of those and monitor his progress. Picking great doctors, I found, is one of the most important things you can do. This is where you want to be a bit picky and do your research!

Chapter 8:

Applied Behavioral Analysis: What we are learning...

In Applied Behavioral Analysis (ABA) therapy, my son learns everyday living skills and how to utilize his skills to function in the world. At age 3, my son transitioned from all the services under early intervention, and we found a great ABA agency covered under our insurance. He learns social, communication, and self-care skills. Through ABA therapy, things that I once thought were impossible became possible. My child was potty-trained by three years old, even without an extensive vocabulary with the help of our BCBA (Board Certified Behavioral Analyst).

I remember feeling overwhelmed that I couldn't properly assist my child with learning skills typical for his age. In ABA, they present a verbal intervention that motivates my son to increase his communication skills. This therapy relies heavily on teamwork. Meaning as caregivers, parents, siblings, and whoever plays a vital role in your child's life, you all have to work together in reinforcing desired behaviors outside of therapy. Our BCBA taught us strategies to assist him through reinforcement and strategies to decrease undesired behaviors.

In ABA, my son learned how to request his wants and needs. We used their techniques in his everyday life events so that he could generalize these behaviors. While I understand ABA therapy is not for everyone, believe me, I was skeptical at first; however, I can whole-heartedly say that it was a game-changer for my son. Looking at how he went from non-verbal to saying 1-2 words and now complete sentences has been a long journey but so amazing to watch.

Here's a list of some of the things ABA assisted with:

- Playing games
- Potty-training
- Daily routine
- Washing hands
- Communication and requesting
- Discussing emotions
- Self-regulating when upset
- Reinforcing appropriate behaviors
- Ignoring undesired behaviors
- Self-care, independence
- Dressing and undressing
- Social skills
- Taking turns
- Acceptance of siblings
- Sharing mom and dad with his sibling

The list continues and is individualized to the needs of your child. If you choose ABA therapy, please do your homework and select a good provider.

CHAPTER 9:

8 TIPS FOR YOUR CHILD'S INDIVIDUALIZED EDUCATIONAL PLAN (IEP)

An Individualized Educational Plan (IEP) is a program designed to meet your child's educational needs throughout their public-school years. The IEP is a goal-orientated document that is very important and helpful towards your child's progress. After your child's diagnosis, this document is needed so that the child is accommodated and the expectations are set for their education. Well, let's take a step back. What helped us transition to public schools and move to the next steps of getting an IEP was the early intervention program. Our service coordinator in the intervention program set up a meeting months before my son turned three years old. Remember, early intervention services end at age 3. The meeting included representatives from the public-school board, schools with ASD programs, and the professionals who completed the evaluations for my son (in our case, there was a speech pathologist and occupational therapist present). The first IEP document was completed at this meeting.

Before the IEP document was created, the early intervention program created an Individualized Family Service Plan (IFSP) at the start of the early intervention program, which every child receives. For my child, we had him evaluated around the age of 20-21 months old when we first noticed certain behaviors; however, you can start anywhere from birth to age 36 months. The IFSP is a document prepared by your child's team of specialists (including you) to develop a plan to assist you and your child. The IFSP process includes you, family members, the service coordinator, therapists, and other professionals who provide early intervention services. This document clearly lays out your child's services and the results you wish to receive. It's important to note that the IFSP ends when your child turns three-years-old along with all their early intervention services such as speech or occupational therapy. Early intervention also helped get my child enrolled in the public-school system's Exceptional Student Education Learning program, which helps with his educational needs. As the IFSP end, the IEP begins.

When entering the public-school system, your child will need an IEP. Don't worry; if your child is enrolled in the early intervention program, your service coordinator sets up this initial step. The IEP can include support services such as speech therapy, occupational therapy, and additional test-taking time. The IEP gives personal goals for your child to meet and addresses how those goals will be attained. It should be written very precisely and specific. When starting public school, be sure to know who your child's Exceptional Student Education (ESE) specialist is as, more than likely, this will be the person who will be scheduling the meetings.

Don't fret; if your child was not enrolled in Early Intervention by age 3, you can contact their education office at their school, and they will assist you in having your child evaluated for an IEP. A teacher may suggest that your child be evaluated but know that they cannot evaluate your child without your consent. You will be given lots of information on the IEP process, but I recommend doing your own research.

8 Tips to get the most out of your child's IEP:

1. Be Honest. If you feel your child has a deficit in certain areas, let the IEP team know.
2. Let your child's strengths and weaknesses be known.
3. Be available to attend every meeting. Let teachers and staff know who you are.

4. Support inclusion. Just like it's essential for your child to get their services, it's just as crucial for them to be around typical children their age.
5. Invite other private therapists who are working with your child to attend the meeting to give their input.
6. Act on the things discussed and ask questions if you need clarification. Read over the document to get a clear understanding.
7. Attend "Navigating the IEP" meetings in your community to gain ideas from others and possibly offer assistance.
8. Breathe! You are not alone in this journey. It's so easy to feel overwhelmed. I promise you will get through it.

Chapter 10:

Adding a Sibling to the Equation

When my son was 3-years-old, my fiancé and I found out we were expecting. Before this, we made a silent pact that we would not have any more children due to our son needing the majority of our attention. Speaking to other parents of children diagnosed with ASD about this subject, we received mixed feedback. Some said that they would never have any more children, while others said it was the best decision they made. I honestly understood both views.

Before finding out we were pregnant with our baby girl, our lives were just starting to settle, and we were in a good routine. We had it all worked out from taking our son to his therapies, having full-time jobs, and going on vacations, amongst other activities. In all honesty, at first, we were terrified about the what-ifs? What if she needed therapy also? What if she's diagnosed? How could we ensure they would both get their needs met? Well, our precious little girl was born on New Year's Eve and has been a blessing ever since.

Her birth was what we needed to complete our family. Going against some of the doctor's statements that my body was not made to have more children due to my hemophilia and I should not attempt to have more, I knew this pregnancy was a blessing, just like with my son. Not to mention, it felt so good to prove them wrong. The way our daughter challenges us as parents to think about things in a different light is incredible. Our two children have become best friends and are so protective of each other. They also have the typical sibling rivalry days when they compete for our attention or do not feel like sharing each other's toys. They copy and learn from one another every day. It's so amazing to see how they interact with each other. Although she doesn't have autism, she has assisted in his social and communication skills tremendously by just doing everyday activities.

Early after her birth, we continued to look for signs of autism, but we eventually realized that she did not show any. Honestly, even if she were, we would ensure she progressed just as our son has.

What I learned from adding a sibling to the equation:

Each child must have their own separate identities. One may have a love for music, while the other(s) may love building things. Celebrate their accomplishments (big or small) and spend time with your children, both together and one-on-one. For example, take one child out for ice cream, and the next day plan to take your other child to do something special they enjoy. It is easy to be consumed with your child's therapies, so be sure you give all your children their special attention. At times you may see some usual sibling envy, but assure your children that they all have a piece of your heart.

Chapter 11:

Things I wish I knew as a new parent

As a new parent (before our son was born), there are many things I wish I had known and pushed myself to do more of. Here are some of the things I sort of regret not doing right away:

- Read, Read, Read to your baby.
- Be silly and do pretend play with them.
- Play peek-a-boo and patty-cake games
- Sing nursery rhymes and create your own songs
- Describe things to your child while you are doing them
- Have play dates
- Participate in Mommy & Me or Daddy & Me classes
- Don't be afraid to accept help.
- Ignore negativity
- Don't allow fear to get in your way of trying new things.
- Join a music movement class with your child
- Don't allow family and friends to talk you out of things because they are not ordinary things from your culture.

Remember that no two children are alike, so do not compare your child to other children even if they are the same age. Someone told me a long time ago, "If you meet someone with autism, you've met someone with autism." That means no two people diagnosed with ASD will show the same behaviors and skills. Your child is different than the next child. One of the main things that make your child different is that they have YOU. You will be their voice and advocate if you allow yourself to be.

People are going to talk. Some won't agree with the decisions you make, say ignorant things, or give crazy stares. I've encountered them all. While out at events, I've experienced the situations previously mentioned, but I had to learn that my child and family belong just like anyone else's child. I can only wish that acceptance and understanding are taught even to adults.

As a parent, be sure to have a Will and a good amount of life insurance. Life insurance is so important! If anything happens to you, you want it to be clear who will serve as a legal guardian for your child. Please discuss this with the person beforehand and place it in your Will. With a life insurance policy, you want to leave wealth for your child to have access to set them up for a better future in their adulthood. Of course, no one wants to think about death and the fact that we all leave this place one day, but this is a reality that is inevitable for us all.

Even if you don't have any children, please get life insurance ASAP! Remember, even the most basic burial services can put others in a financial bind, and no one should be burdened with unexpected costs, especially your children.

Honestly, it took me some time to settle down and get both a term and whole life insurance policy, especially after the incident following my gallbladder surgery. Before, I only had what was provided through my employers. Everywhere I've worked, I had a life insurance policy, so I thought I was safe. I had a reality check that reminded me that I would no longer be covered under their life insurance plan if I was ever to leave the job. You just have to do your homework and find what's affordable. My suggestion is to get a term and whole life policy.

Lastly, I recommend you research other programs, events, and festivities in your community that may aid in your child's development. Every month, maybe twice a month after my daughter was born, we went to different community events. Some we found online, postings at his school, and through our city's advertisement magazines. We learned how critical social skills were and are for my son, so the more we exposed him and placed him in these environments, the more comfortable he became.

CHAPTER 12:

YOU CAN'T POUR FROM AN EMPTY CUP.

Parents and caregivers, I know that it is very easy to be overly involved in our children's lives because we want the very best for them, but you must make self-care a priority. Taking care of yourself is most important, and it is something I had to drill into my head repeatedly. How can I care for my children if I'm not adequately caring for myself? Having good physical, emotional and mental health should not be a luxury.

How will you transfer good energy to those who depend on you if you are emotionally weak? We have to implement into our schedule, finding time to do what we love doing outside of caregiving. If that's reading a book, swimming, skating, having a date night, developing a business plan, going to see a movie, or going out for ice cream, whatever it may be, just do it without feeling any guilt. With all the therapies your child may have, it is vital to still have your "me time" in the midst of it all. Know that you are the best and you are doing your best!

The most important thing about this journey was our faith. We believed in the power of prayer and also lived by the words of "having faith without work is dead." Having faith, being positive, and doing the work is what helps us each day. Through this, we've seen endless possibilities. There will be moments in this process that will be hard, extremely hard. Don't give up! If you have to take a break, do that! Love on your child but also love on yourself too!

Appendix I:

Question & Answers Unpacking a Bit More

Question:

What are some of the signs I saw in my son that made me assume he may have autism?

Answer:

Regression in eye contact, flapping of hands, and tip-toe walking. Parents and caregivers, please do not be alarmed if your child is exhibiting these behaviors, but if you are concerned, please seek early intervention. There is no harm in getting your child evaluated.

Question:

Do I tell my family and/or friends that my son has been diagnosed with autism spectrum disorder? How do I tell them?

Answer:

Okay, this is a tricky one. My suggestion is to tell them once you feel comfortable talking about it. You have to be ready to answer some of their questions and be prepared that many people don't understand ASD and may come off as insensitive or even ignorant. If you choose to tell them, make it simple. Let them know how you are feeling and if you don't want to be bombarded with a million questions, let them know that.

It took me a long time to talk about my son's diagnosis with my family. At times I was even thinking about how that conversation would commence caused me to break down in tears. Yes, I received many "odd" reactions, but I also received a lot of support. Use your instincts and let your heart decide. Remember to tell your family and friends to treat your child just like they would treat other children and try not to single them out.

Question:

I want to enroll my child in sports or other extracurricular activities. Do I look for programs that accept only children with ASD or other developmental delays?

Answer:

Absolutely not! Look for programs that support inclusion. You want your child to be around all children. Remember that children mimic other children, so your child being around other typical children will help their development. When my son was three years old, we began to enroll him in t-ball, and he played so well with all the children. It was a program that accepted all children from all backgrounds. We were so nervous as parents, but in the end, it was so worth it. He flourished in each game and did very well, learning to play the sport. It was amazing to see him having fun and starting to focus on the different techniques.

Question:

My child is sensitive to sounds. Should I shy away from going to activities that have distinctive sounds?

Answer:

You have to treat this one on a case-by-case scenario. For example, my son was very sensitive to the sounds of fireworks. I wanted him to enjoy the bright colors and sparklers produced by the fireworks, but also I wanted him to feel safe to know that this is a fun event. We learned to start small before progressing to huge events such as the Fourth of July fireworks show. We brought sparklers and poppers and showed him how fun they were. We watched videos from past firework events and played the volume on low, and gradually increased it. This was a slow process, but now he gets so excited when seeing them.

I would not necessarily shy away from any event without first trying to de-sensitize your child. Remember, change does not occur overnight, so be very patient. If it works great and if it doesn't work, at least you all tried. Please don't write it off too soon, though. You can re-visit it later and try again.

Question:

How can I assist my child with riding a bike?

Answer:

We purchased a balance bike and gave him lots of praise. Many children with autism have a hard time balancing, so the balance bike was perfect for him to master first. Trying to balance and pedal at the same time was hard. The balance bike gears their attention to just being able to work on balancing. We taught him about stopping, noticing stop signs, and crossing the street on the balance bike. When your child is ready, you can move them to a bike with pedals. After mastering the balance bike, my son was promoted to a bike with pedals and training wheels. Before we knew it, he was pedaling up and down the neighborhood on his bike.

Question:

How can I prepare my child for the dentist?

Answer:

Research or ask other parents for a dentist who specializes in treating children with autism. Our son goes to a dentist specializing in dentistry for children with autism, and we learned about him after attending an open house at his school. My son's dentist developed a transition plan to introduce him to dental instruments so he doesn't feel overwhelmed at each visit. We were given a cartoon video and picture story of what to expect during the visit. The illustrations on the video showed pictures of the actual dentist, dental assistants, and the office itself. On our first two visits to the dentist's office, our BCBA attended the appointments with us for support.

The dentist incorporates ABA and a Picture Exchange Communication System (PECS) in each visit so that he can understand the next steps. In our journey, I've learned to select health professionals who have experience working with children with ASD. Believe me; you'll save yourself the headache of hopping around to different health professionals.

Question:

How do I prepare my child for new adventures/outings such as going to the movies, circus, carnival, or a puppet show?

Answer:

We learned to show our child a video or picture of that specific activity in the weeks leading up to the event. You also want to have conversations about it so they understand and begin to feel at ease when you arrive at an event. For example, if you are going to the circus, then show them videos of an actual circus and start talking about things they will see and may experience.

Question:

How can I assist my child with properly holding a crayon, marker, or pencil?

Answer:

Use broken crayons or broken pencils. This will force their fingers to grip the writing tool properly. You should also refer to an occupational therapist to assist you with techniques.

Question:

How do I assist my child(ren) with performing a preferred task versus a non-preferred task?

Answer:

Presenting your child with praise and positive reinforcers can make a huge difference. I remember how difficult it was for my son to learn how to eat with a fork and spoon. In occupational therapy, they worked with him on learning to use utensils, but the real task came when he was at home. His dad and I learned to praise him for every little attempt to use his utensils and slowly faded away from the praise after mastering each task.

This also went for other preferred tasks such as potty-training, learning to wash his hands, drinking from a straw, etc. Finding what form of reinforcers will work for your child can range from easy to difficult, but who knows your child better than you. Believe me; you will figure it out.

Question:

Outside of therapy, what can I do to help my child progress?

Answer:

Purchase some toys without the bells and whistles. When selecting toys for your child, be sure that they promote gross and fine motor skills. I've learned that many toy companies place labels on their boxes stating what skill/development their toy will promote for your child, but many of those claims are unfounded. Selecting some toys without loud sounds and bright lights should be your go-to toys. I'm not saying that you should shy away from those types of toys with a distinctive music and sounds but create a nice balance. We purchased wooden toys, building toys, and others that require the use of problem-solving skills. When my son became toddler-age and learned about the on/off switch on his toys, we used it to promote communication. We'd switch his toys to the off mode, and because his little fingers were not strong enough at the time, he'd find us and begin to use non-verbal techniques to request/ask us to switch his toy to the on-position. This was not easy because he'd get very irritable at times, but in the end, he learned to requests things he wanted.

Labels things around your house and in their room to their eye level. This will not only increase their vocabulary, but they will learn to pair words and actions. Select products that promote pretend play, such as dolls, trucks, play kitchen sets, child-sized cleaning tools, etc. Finally, let your child have fun, go on playdates or join activities/sports.

Question:

If you can state the most important key to parenting a child with autism, what would it be?

Answer:

Consistency in following a routine. Following a daily routine and reminding your child of the next activity that will take place will make your day structured and help them with calming their anxieties. Many children with autism have a fear of commencing new activities or encountering things outside of their routine. Making a schedule of what will take place and when it will take place is helpful. For example, when school ends, my son comes home and has a 1-hour break (30 minutes is spent on his tablet and 30 minutes spent doing any screen-free activities). After that hour break, ABA therapy starts, let's say from 2:30 pm – 6:30 pm; he has free time for an additional half-hour after ABA ends and then its reading time. We have tons of books, and we ask him to pick out three books he'd like to read. After dinnertime is complete, we prepare for bedtime, which includes taking a bath, brushing teeth, and setting out his clothes for the next day. It's important to note that each of these activities has its own time slot and that we are communicating with him at least 5 minutes before the current activity ends. We say things like, "Okay, five more minutes of using your tablet, then you have to turn it off. You can play a game, do a puzzle, or another activity of your choice."

Appendix II:

My Promise to Myself as a Caregiver

Write down three self-care tasks that you are going to engage in. Each month make this dedication to yourself to commit to 3 personal tasks. A simple list like the one listed below would suffice.

Month: _____

_____

_____

_____

Write it somewhere such as a sticky note on your desk, the refrigerator, or on the mirror. You owe yourself this. Remember, self-care is a priority in unpacking the puzzle.

www.ingramcontent.com/pod-product-compliance
Lightning Source LLC
Chambersburg PA
CBHW071416290426
44108CB00014B/1848